S0-ANR-051

Green Means Go

by Susan Ring

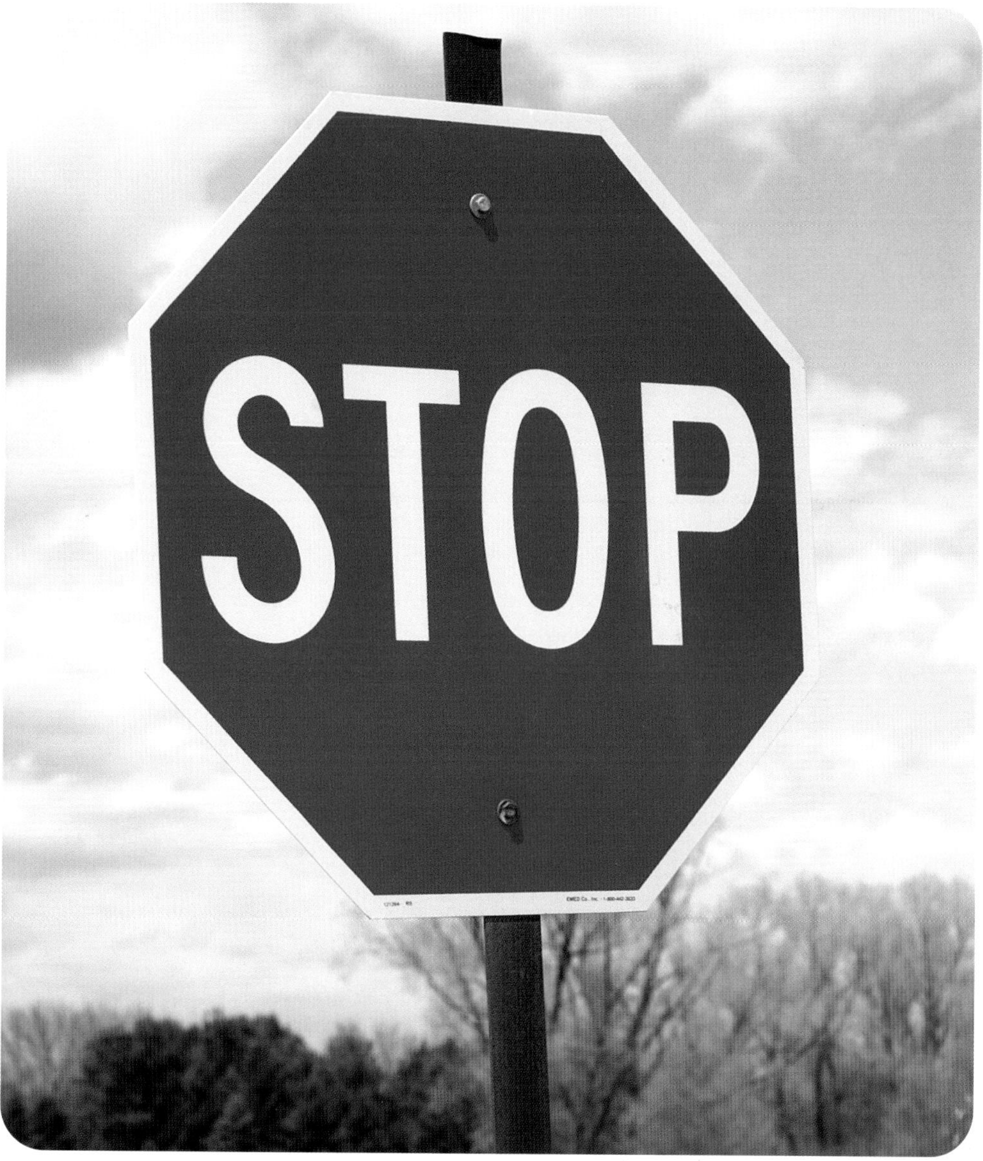

Red means stop.

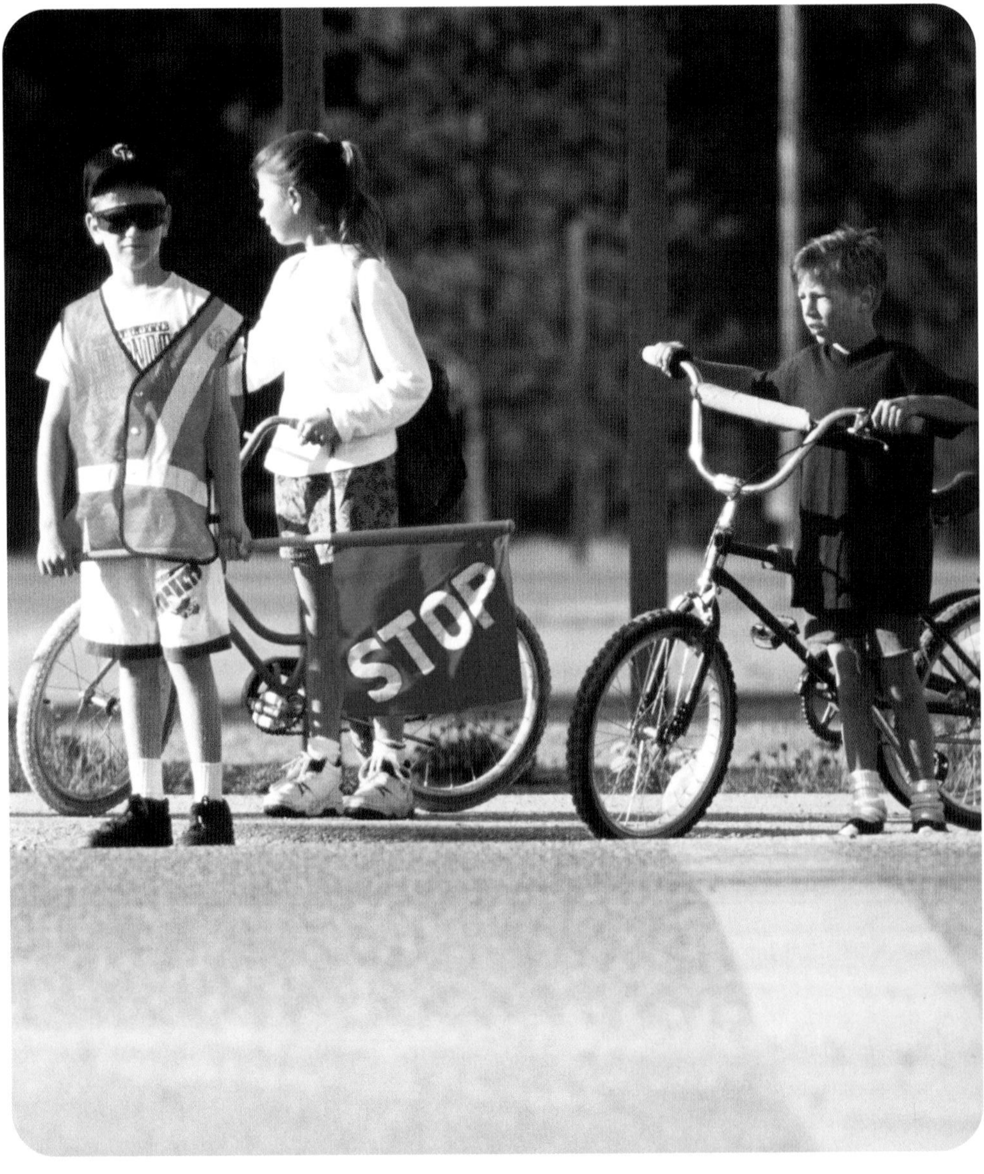

Green means go.

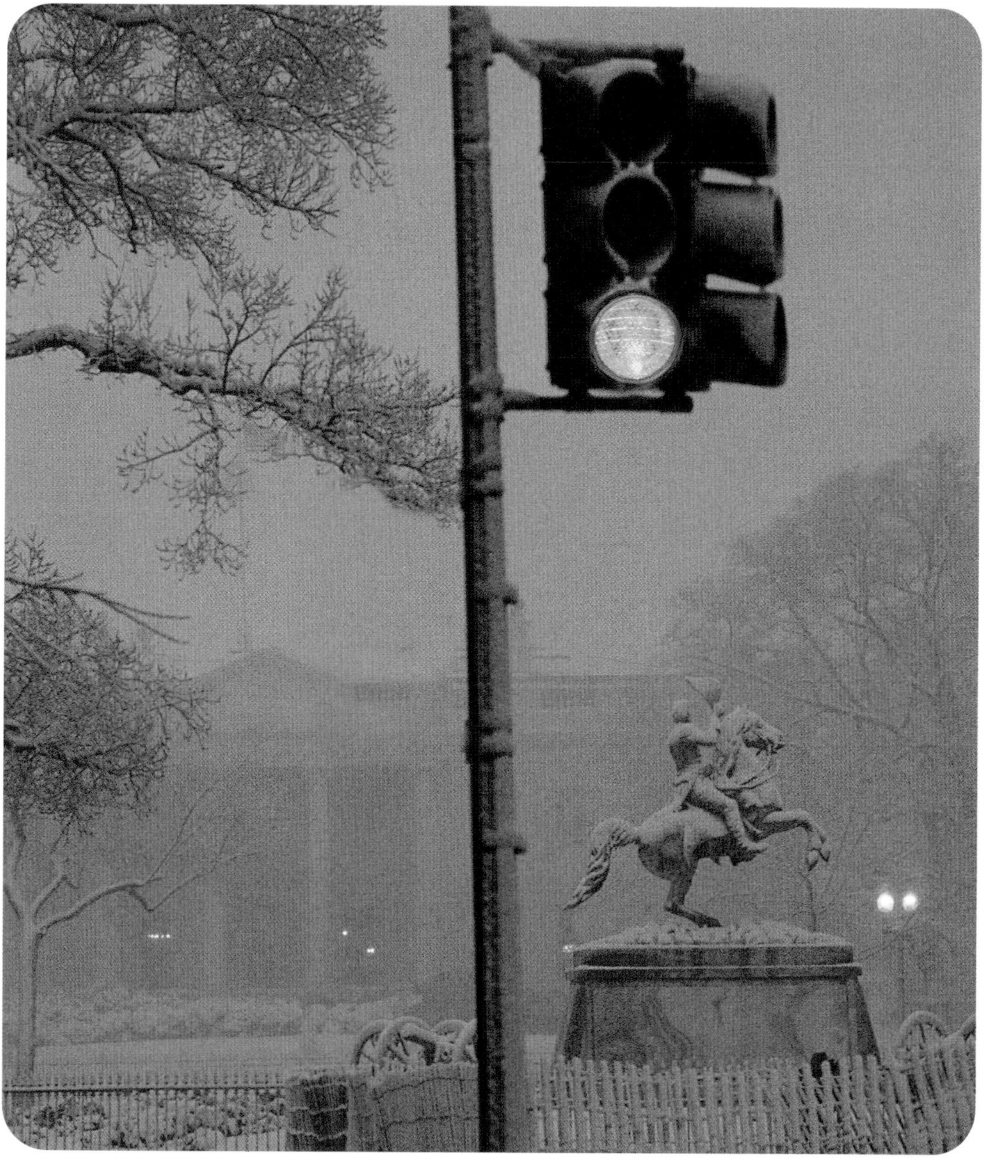

Yellow means to go real slow.

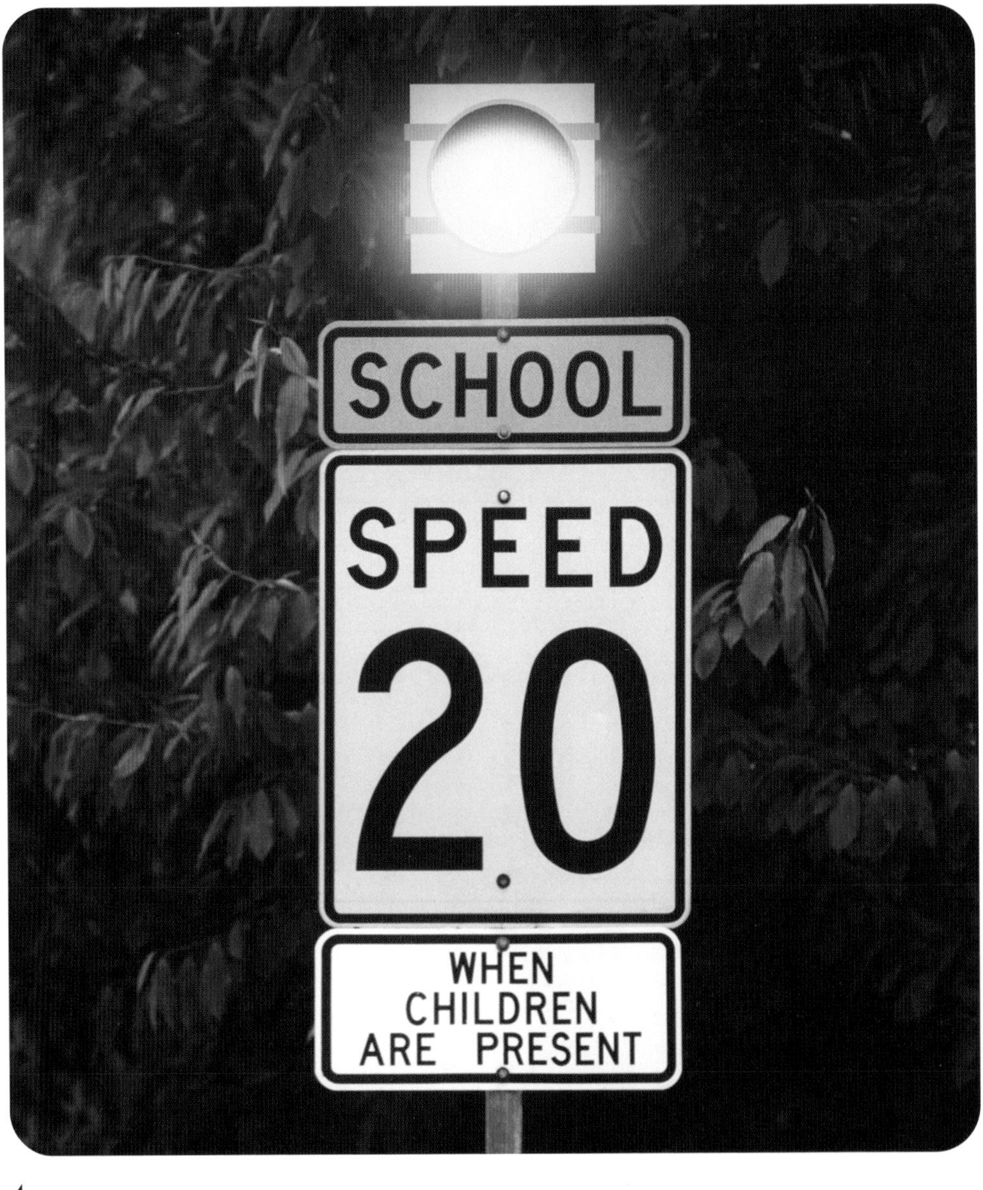

When we ride

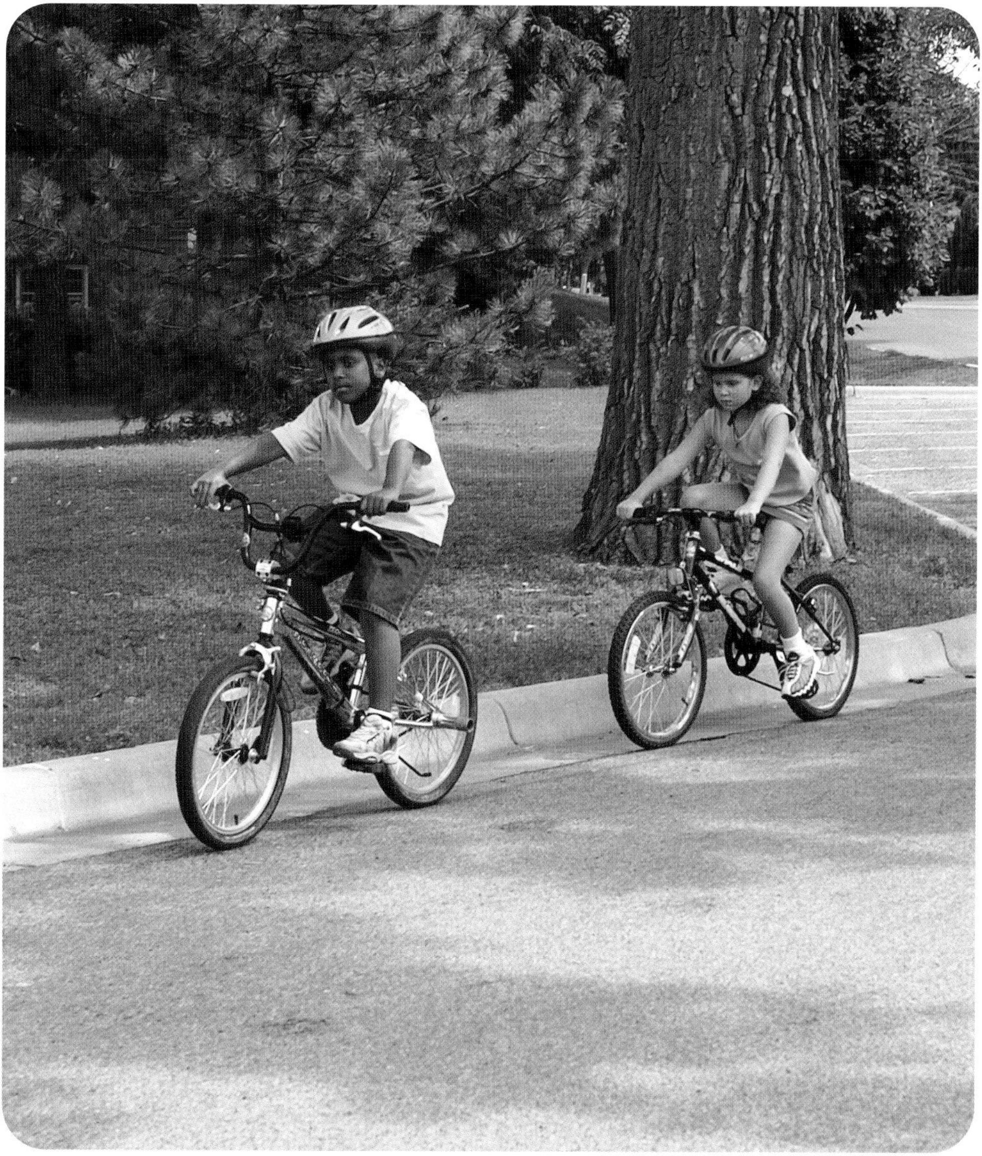

and when we play,

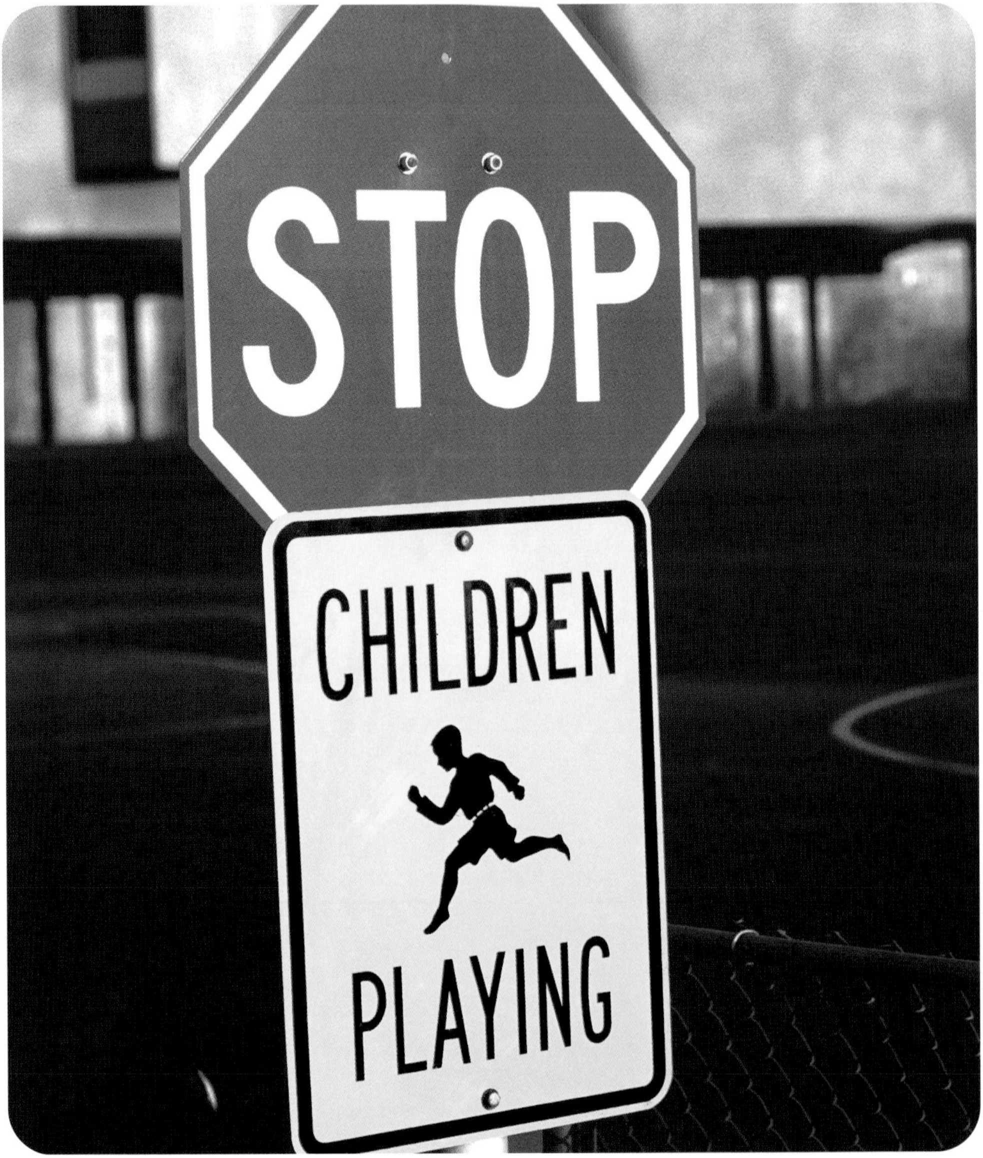

these rules help us

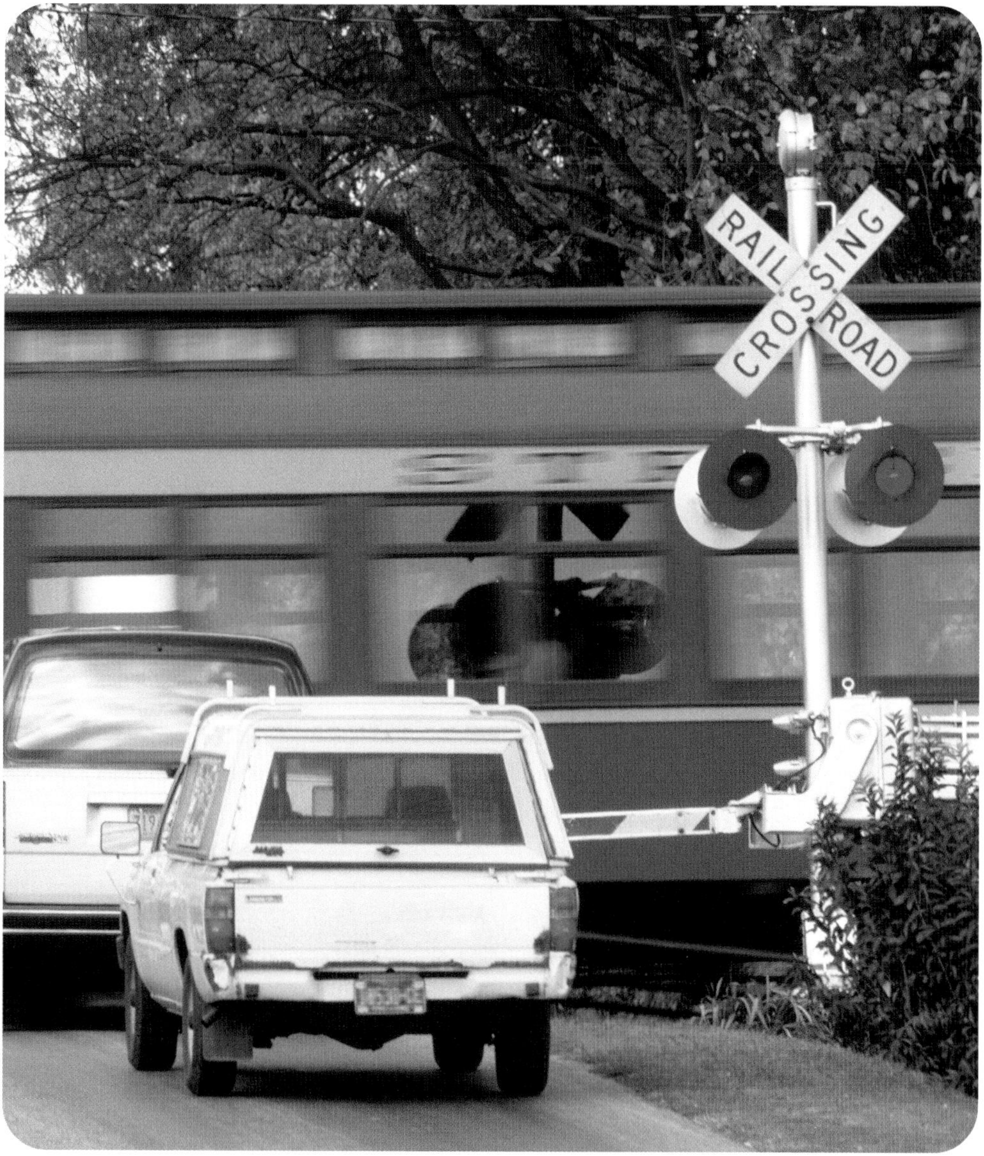

every day.

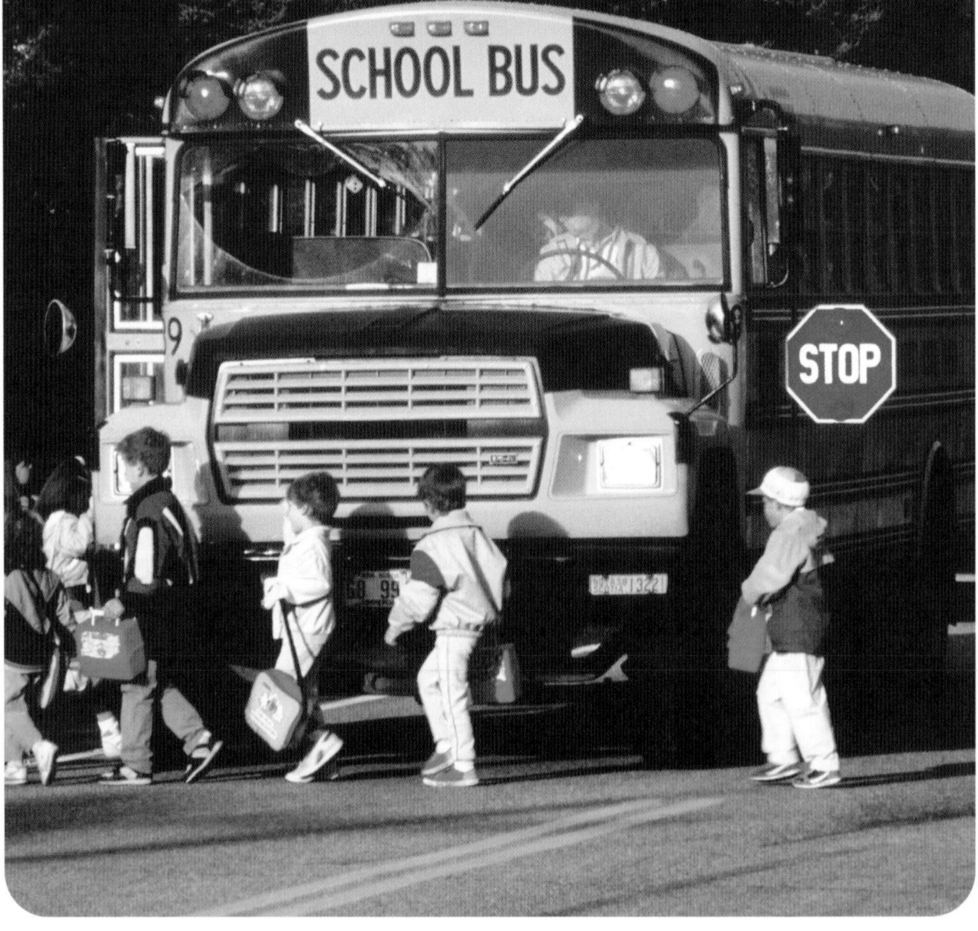
SCHOOL BUS
STOP